ANIMALS

Snails

by Kevin J. Holmes

Content Consultant:
Dr. Eugene P. Keferl
Professor of Biology
Coastal Georgia Community College

Bridgestone Books
an imprint of Capstone Press

Bridgestone Books are published by Capstone Press
818 North Willow Street, Mankato, Minnesota 56001
http://www.capstone-press.com

Library of Congress Cataloging-in-Publication Data
Holmes, Kevin J.
    Snails/by Kevin J. Holmes.
    p. cm.--(Animals)
    Includes bibliographical references (p. 23) and index.
    Summary: An introduction to snails' physical characteristics,
habits, behavior, and relationships to humans.
    ISBN 1-56065-746-4
    1. Snails--Juvenile literature. [1. Snails.] I. Title. II. Series: Holmes, Kevin J. Animals.
QL430.4.H65 1998
593'.3--dc21

                           97-31852
                             CIP
                             AC

Editorial credits:
Editor, Martha E. Hillman; cover design, Timothy Halldin; photo research, Michelle L. Norstad

Photo credits:
James H. Robinson, 4, 18
Connie Toops, 12
Unicorn Stock Photos/A. Gurmankin, cover; Charles E. Schmidt, 6; Dick Keen, 14
Visuals Unlimited/Hal Beral, 8; John D. Cunningham, 10; Dave B. Fleetham, 16;
  W. J. Weber, 20

Table of Contents

Fast Facts

Kinds: There are more than 60,000 kinds of snails.

Range: Snails live everywhere in the world.

Habitat: Snails live in ponds, deserts, and rivers. They live in oceans, mountains, and woods.

Food: Snails eat living plants, rotting plants, and water plants. Some eat small animals.

Mating: Many snails mate in the spring. Some snails can mate at any time of year.

Young: Young snails hatch from eggs. Most hatch as young adult snails. Some hatch as larvas. Larvas are snails in a growing stage. They grow into adult snails.

Snails

Snails are mollusks. A mollusk has a soft body and no backbone. Mollusks usually have slippery skin. Hard shells often cover most of their skin.

Snails are also gastropods. Gastropod means stomach foot. A snail does not have legs. It moves on its stomach. People call a snail's stomach its foot.

Snails leave trails of slime behind them when they move. The slime helps them move smoothly from place to place. The slime also keeps their soft bodies from being cut.

There are more than 60,000 kinds of snails in the world. They live on land and in water. They live in warm and cold areas.

The largest snails in the world are Australian trumpet snails. They grow up to 2.5 feet (80 centimeters) long. The smallest snails are smaller than the head of a pin.

Some snails live on land.

Appearance

Without their shells, most snails would look alike. Their bodies are soft and slimy.

A snail's foot is the largest uncovered part of its body. A snail's foot is a long, flat muscle. Snails use this muscle to move around.

A snail's head is at the front of its foot. A snail's eyes, mouth, and tentacles are on its head. A tentacle is a long, armlike body part. Animals use tentacles for feeling objects around them.

Snails have one pair of tentacles. Some snails have a pair of eye stalks. An eye stalk is a tentacle with an eye at the tip. Snails cannot see well. They can only tell the difference between light and darkness.

Snail shells are many shapes, colors, and sizes. Some shells look like cones or long screws. Some shells have sharp points. Many shells are bright colors. Others are dull colors.

Some snail shells are bright colors.

Homes

Snails live everywhere in the world. They live on land, in freshwater, and in the ocean. Freshwater is water without salt. Ocean water has salt in it.

Land snails live in wet, cool places. Most snails dry up and die without water. Many land snails live by water in the woods.

Freshwater snails live in ponds, marshes, lakes, and rivers. A marsh is an area of low, wet land.

Some ocean snails live in shallow water near shore. Shallow means not deep. Others live in the deep waters away from land.

Most snails cannot live in very hot or very cold climates. They like to live where it is warm and wet. But some snails live in deserts.

Many North American snails hibernate during the winter. Hibernate means to spend the winter in a deep sleep.

Some ocean snails live in shallow water near shore.

Shells

A snail does not outgrow its shell. Its shell grows larger as its body grows.

A snail's hard shell grows slowly out of its mantle. A mantle is a thin skin. It covers a snail's body under its shell.

The growing part of a shell is the lip. The lip is the edge of a shell closest to a snail's head.

A snail can hide in its shell to stay safe. Part of a snail's body is always inside its shell. Each snail shell has an opening near the lip. Most snails can pull their entire bodies inside the shell. They do this when they are in danger.

Some snails have operculums. An operculum is a plate on the bottom of a snail's foot. Operculums seal the shells when snails pull inside.

Snails hide in their shells to stay safe.

Food

Most snails are herbivores. A herbivore is an animal that eats plants. Land snails eat grass, leaves, and rotting plants. Freshwater snails eat algae and other water plants. Algae are small, floating plants. Ocean snails eat seaweed.

Some snails are carnivores. A carnivore is an animal that eats meat. These snails eat small fish and other snails. They also eat small dead animals.

Snails have radulas. A radula is a long, flat tongue. A radula is covered with tiny, sharp teeth. Snails use radulas to eat. Snails rub plants and animals with their radulas. This loosens pieces of food. Then snails pull the food into their mouths.

Land snails eat grass, leaves, and rotting plants.

Enemies

Many predators eat snails. A predator is an animal that hunts other animals for food.

Birds, insects, frogs, and other animals eat land snails. Some birds reach inside snails' shells and pull out snails' bodies. Other birds drop shells against rocks until they break open.

Fish, ducks, turtles, frogs, and birds eat freshwater snails. Crabs, fish, other snails, and whales eat ocean snails.

Many snails have camouflaged shells. Camouflage is coloring that makes something look like its surroundings. Camouflage helps snails stay safe. Predators cannot easily see snails that look like their surroundings.

Many snails have camouflaged shells.

Young Snails

Land snails lay their eggs about four weeks after mating. Mate means to join together to produce young. They lay about 50 eggs in damp soil.

Freshwater and ocean snails make a jelly. They lay their eggs in the jelly. They stick their eggs on plants or stones.

Snails hatch from the eggs. Most look like adult snails. But their shells are thin and soft. Their shells harden and grow as they age.

Some snails hatch as larvas. A larva is an animal in a growing stage. Some larvas do not have shells. They float in the water and sink to the bottom. They eat plants. They grow into young snails with shells.

Snails hatch from eggs.

Snails and People

Snails help people by keeping soil and water healthy. Snails eat rotting plants and algae. Their waste makes soil rich. Plants grow well in rich soil.

Some snails harm crops. Many farmers poison snails to keep them from eating crops. People who raise oysters and clams must remove snails. Snails eat young oysters and clams.

People catch and eat snails. Many restaurants around the world serve snails. Some people collect snail shells.

Some people kill insects with poisons. The poisons wash into lakes and rivers where snails live. These poisons destroy the snails' homes.

Many countries have laws that help snails. It is illegal to catch large snails in some places. Other laws keep snails' homes safe.

Snails help people by keeping soil and water healthy.

Hands On: Snail Slime

Snails leave trails of slime behind them when they move. You can make your own slime.

What You Need

1 cup corn starch
1 cup water

Sand paper
Food coloring

Bowl
Spoon

What You Do

1. Put the corn starch in a bowl.
2. Add the water.
3. Add several drops of food coloring.
4. Stir with the spoon until the items are mixed.
5. Slide your dry hand along the sand paper.
6. Put some slime on the sand paper. Now slide your hand through the slime. The slime helps your hand move smoothly.

Snails use slime to move smoothly from place to place. The slime also keeps their soft bodies from being cut.

Words to Know

camouflage (KAM-uh-flahzh)—coloring that makes something look like its surroundings

herbivore (HUR-buh-vor)—an animal that eats plants

hibernate (HYE-bur-nate)—to spend the winter in a deep sleep

mantle (MAN-tuhl)—a thin skin that covers a snail's body under its shell

mollusk (MOL-uhsk)—an animal with a soft body and no backbone

operculum (oh-PUR-kyuh-lum)—a plate on the bottom of a snail's foot

radula (RA-juh-luh)—a long, flat tongue covered with tiny, sharp teeth

tentacle (TEN-tuh-kuhl)—a long, armlike body part

Read More

Fisher, Enid. *Snails*. Milwaukee: Gareth Stevens, 1996.

Stone, Lynn M. *Slugs and Snails*. Vero Beach, Fla.: Rourke Book Co., 1995.

Useful Addresses

**Florida Museum of
  Natural History—Malacology**
University of Florida
Gainesville, FL 32611-7800

**Hawaiian Malacological
  Society**
P.O. Box 22130
Honolulu, HI 96823-2130

Internet Sites

Conchologists of America—Things To Do
http://coa.acnatsci.org/conchnet/do.html
The Giant African Land Snail Page
http://www.igor.demon.co.uk/snail.htm
Snails
http://ast.leeds.ac.uk/~agg/snails.html

Index